Hypnosis

Hypnosis Beginners Guide: Learn How To Use Hypnosis To Relieve Stress, Anxiety, Depression and Become Happier

Richard Cooper

Table of Contents

INTRODUCTION

I want to thank you and congratulate you for purchasing the book, *"Hypnosis Beginners Guide: Learn How To Use Hypnosis To Relieve Stress, Anxiety, Depression and Become Happier"*.

This book has actionable information on how to use hypnosis to overcome stress, depression and to live a happy life.

What comes to mind at the mention of hypnosis? Is it the hypnosis sessions you see on movies where someone is made to sort of behave like a zombie because they have no control over what they do or not do? I cannot blame you for that especially because the media has made hypnosis seem like some form of spell that someone casts on another to make them have full control over their will.

Well, when most people hear the word hypnosis, they associate it with the supernatural or someone taking control away from them but is that really the truth? There are also those who do not know the difference between hypnosis and meditation and probably believe that the two are just the same thing.

Whatever it is, hypnosis has been used for many years to help people heal and become a better version of themselves. It has helped people overcome addictions, extreme pain, restlessness and even in dealing with past issues that were affecting their present life like stress, phobias, anxiety, depression and others. Do you want to unleash the full power of hypnosis to get all its benefits in your daily life? Well, if you do, this book will help you to learn a lot about hypnosis and how you can use it to deal with some of the problems you've been struggling with for years.

In this book, you will get to know what hypnosis is, its benefits, how different it is from meditation and most importantly, you will get to know how to do it by yourself so that you are never afraid given that you will be hypnotizing yourself at will. While it does take some work to master how to hypnotize yourself at will, the benefits that you get are well worth the struggle.

Thanks again for purchasing this book, I hope you enjoy it!

CHAPTER 1

HYPNOSIS: THE BASICS

History of Hypnosis

Hypnosis is not exactly a new concept. People have been entering into hypnotic-type trances for several years- we are talking about thousands and thousands of years ago. In many cultures and religions, it was regarded as a form of meditation.

Modern day hypnosis however started in the late 1700s and was made popular by Franz Mesmer, an Austrian physician who became known as the father of 'modern hypnotism'. In fact, hypnosis used to be known as 'Mesmerism' as it was named after Franz Mesmer.

Mesmer held the opinion that hypnosis was a sort of mystical force that flows from the hypnotist to the person being hypnotized but his theory was dismissed by critics who asserted that there was no magical element to hypnotism.

Before long, hypnotism started finding its way into the world of modern medicine. The use of hypnotism in the medical field was made popular by Surgeons and physicians like John Elliotson and James Esdaille and researchers like James Braid who helped to reveal the biological and physical benefits of hypnotism.

Thanks to their persistence and efforts, it wasn't long before hypnotism became accepted as a valid clinical technique and started to be taught as a course in schools and universities and offered as a form of therapy for treatment of some health conditions in hospitals.

What Is Hypnosis

In its simplest terms, hypnosis is a trance state, which is usually characterized by extreme relaxation, suggestibility, and heightened imagination, which is far different from sleep because you are actually alert. It is something close to daydreaming or a state in which you feel as if you are losing yourself in a movie or book while you are fully conscious but out of tune to much of the external stimuli around you except the subject at hand.

When you are in this state, you sort of have no other thought going on in your mind. You can think of it like using a magnifying glass to focus on the rays of the sun in order to make them a lot more powerful. As such, hypnosis is like having concentrated and focused attention (think of how you use a magnifying glass to concentrate and focus the sunrays) in order to make use of our mind a lot more powerfully. In other words, with hypnosis, you can use your mind to achieve feats that you wouldn't be able to do in your non-hypnotic state. You are able to tap into the mind's limitless power to unleash more potential from you.

When you are in a hypnosis session, you view the suggestions that the hypnotist makes or your own ideas as the reality. In this case, if you (or the hypnotist) suggest(s) that your tongue has swollen and is now twice its normal size, you believe it and feel the full sensation of a swollen tongue including having trouble when speaking. And if they suggest that you are drinking chocolate milkshake, you taste it in your mouth and feel its taste and cooling effect in your mouth and down your throat. And if they suggest that you are now experiencing fear, you start feeling panicky and even start exhibiting all the symptoms of fear. But through all that time, you know that everything you are doing is just in your mind (imaginary). So essentially, you are sort of 'playing pretend' on a completely advanced level where you feel everything as you would normally feel if the real thing were to happen.

When you are in a trance state, you feel uninhibited and completely relaxed probably because it is at this time when you have tuned out all your doubts and worries, which often keep your actions in check. You feel as if you are engrossed in a movie plot with no worries about work, family, and money and others such that you cannot move your focus elsewhere; your mind and body are 100% present! You are also highly suggestible so if you or the hypnotist suggest(s) something, you comply without asking questions. This part is probably what makes hypnosis interesting (and what the media tends to focus more on) where you see normally reserved and sensible adults doing some things that they wouldn't do when 'sober' because all embarrassment seems to have flown out of the window.

Well, for starters, this is not like what you see in the movies. Hypnosis refers to a natural state of selected and focused attention. This simply means that there is no supernatural activities involved; hypnosis is 100% natural. Even though this whole process is naturally normal, it is still one thing that fascinates people about the human mind. We have a unique way of entering this one of a kind state of consciousness and therefore have a gateway to many possibilities of exploration of self, change, and healing. Different generations have used this for thousands of years (especially in religious practices). Science picked it up around 1700 from the father of modern hypnosis Franz Mesmer.

If you are in a state of hypnosis (trance), you can use your thoughts, experiences, and even abilities in ways that are usually impossible when conscious. It is in this state that you are able to develop individual abilities from within you that empower you to make the desired changes in your thinking, feelings, and even behaviors. It cannot be explained but hypnosis can empower you to make intentional changes automatically, changes that would be so hard to make consciously.

For instance, you can use it to treat pain, depression, stress, anxiety, habit disorders, and so many other psychological and medical issues. This however does not mean that hypnosis offers a solution to every psychological problem.

Note: Hypnosis is only recommended after consultations with a qualified health practitioner who has been trained in the use and limitations of medical hypnosis.

Hypnosis is not only limited to clinical use but is also used in research as well with the aim of understanding it deeper as well the impact hypnosis has on sensation, learning, perception, memory and physiology. Researchers are studying the value that hypnosis has in the treatment of physical and psychological health complications.

So the question is how does a treatment aimed at the mind affect the body? Well, your body responds physically to your thoughts. For instance, if you are thinking that you are going to be late for an appointment, you start walking fast or even running. This is the same thing with hypnosis. There are autonomic nervous involuntary systems in the body that can be used to promote good health. When you are in a state of trance, you are more open to suggestions. Therefore, this can be easy to diminish negative physical reactions by bringing in positive suggestions.

Well, while you might think that all hypnosis sessions are identical, they really aren't. But even with this, many myths surround hypnosis. Let's identify some of them and burst them.

Myths About Hypnosis

Many people are scared of hypnosis because of so many scary things that they have heard about hypnosis. These popular misconceptions have caused fear and apprehension in people's minds that they would rather avoid the practice regardless of the benefits it holds for them.

And who would blame them? The movie industry and the media have been largely responsible for these misrepresentations. In most movies where scenes about hypnosis are introduced, you see where a person is controlled to do something odd by another person against his or her will in the name of hypnosis. This is just pure fiction and very far from what hypnosis is about, how it is conducted and what it is used for.

There is a need to debunk some of these myths you might have heard about hypnosis so that you can see and understand that hypnosis is a safe and healthy practice rather than the demonic practice the media makes it seem like.

1. **Hypnosis can be used to control you or force you to do things against your will**

This is a very common but extremely wrong idea of the effects of hypnosis. One fact you must understand about hypnosis is that the hypnotized (You) is always in control and not the hypnotist. It is you who determines your level of participation in the session and no one can actually force you to do anything against your will except you willingly accept to do it. Hypnosis is not a state of sleep where you are unaware of what is going on around you. In fact, it is a state of heightened awareness where you are fully aware of happenings around you.

2. Hypnosis Can Make You Reveal Your Personal Secrets

Another common belief is that while you are being hypnotized, you can be made to reveal your secrets or things that you would rather not share. This is also false because the hypnotist does not have that kind of control over you. All hypnosis is actually self-hypnosis whether you are doing it yourself or with assistance from a professional. If you are not willing to cooperate with the hypnotist on any level, there is little or nothing they can do. The position of the hypnotist is that of a guide and not a slave master. If he makes suggestions that you are not comfortable with, your mind automatically rejects them.

3. Hypnosis is for people with Weak Minds

Some people also confuse being hypnotized with having no will power and as such believe that hypnosis is for people who are weak minded but the opposite is true. Hypnosis requires the ability to concentrate, motivation to cooperate and a lot of intelligence. These are hardly characteristics of weak minded people because people who have low IQ's find it very hard to concentrate on such level.

4. You may be 'trapped' in a Hypnotic State

A lot of first timers ask questions like "what if I'm trapped?", "what if I am unable to wake up?"

This cannot happen because your mind has the capacity to safely pull you out of a state of hypnosis. If during a session, the hypnotists suddenly stops giving commands or talking at all, you would be able to realize this and come out of the hypnosis on your own or you may simply drift up into a brief sleep and then wake up later feeling more refreshed and alert. So with or without the help of the hypnotist, you are able to always come out of hypnosis on your own.

5. Hypnosis is a Dangerous Practice

Hypnosis is mostly safe except in conditions where the person being hypnotized suffers from epilepsy or when the person is operating machinery or driving.

As for people who suffer from epilepsy, hypnosis is bad for them because being in a complete state of relaxation may trigger epileptic seizures. For people driving or operating machines, the reasons are obvious. It may lead to accidents, which may cause danger for them or others around them.

Otherwise, hypnosis is a completely safe and natural process. In fact, hypnosis is something that most people unconsciously do on a daily basis. If you have ever daydreamed before, then you have passed into a hypnotic state or if you have ever been in a situation where you are reading or doing something and you are so absorbed in that thing that you are unaware of your surroundings or anything else around you, that's a light state of hypnosis.

6. Hypnosis is Brainwashing

You should not confuse hypnosis with brainwashing, as they are two entirely different things. Brainwashing occurs when a person goes through extended periods of physical and emotional stress and discomfort that eventually leads to a breakdown. When a person is brainwashed, they begin to act like a robot and accept all commands issued to them without any analytical thinking.

Hypnosis is different because it is a situation where the person being hypnotized is helped to relax and become comfortable. The aim of hypnotist is to achieve cooperation from the client and not blind obedience.

7. Hypnosis Requires Magical Powers

Hypnotism doesn't require any special or magical power. A hypnotist is a regular human being who has received professional training and has fully understood how the human brain responds to and processes information. They have learnt how the subconscious works and they use this knowledge to comfortably guide their clients into a state of hypnosis. There are absolutely no magical or demonic powers involved in hypnotism.

8. You Can Become Addicted to Hypnosis

Hypnosis is a short term and most hypnotists would teach, and hand over the power of hypnosis to their clients so that they are able to perform self-hypnosis on their own. Therefore, you cannot become addicted to hypnosis or to your hypnotist.

Now that you know that all the ugly things you have heard about hypnosis in the past are mostly untrue and hypnosis is actually a safe, healthy and natural process, let's take a quick look at some of the types of hypnosis:

Types of Hypnosis

There are three main types of hypnosis, which are used by hypnotherapists or yourself. A therapist might specialize in one type of hypnosis while some people may respond better to a certain type of hypnosis. These hypnosis types include:

• **Traditional Suggestion Hypnosis**

In this method, an individual is put into a relaxed state known as deeply hypnosis- hypnotherapy. They (hypnotist) then put hypnotic suggestions into your subconscious mind to help you achieve the results you desire.

Of the three methods of hypnosis, this is the easiest and the most commonly used. However, this kind of hypnosis doesn't work for people who are too analytical or logical.

• **Ericksonian Hypnosis**

In this case, the therapist does not place suggestions or commands to the subconscious mind. Instead, they use metaphors to get desired results. The underlying principle in this method is that your subconscious will automatically make a connection between the metaphor and the behavior desired. The metaphor serves as a distraction to the conscious. So, while the conscious brain is busy trying to figure out what the metaphor means, the metaphor's meaning goes straight to the subconscious.

This type of hypnosis is effective on people who are highly logical, critical, or resistant to the idea of being hypnotized.

- **Neuro-Linguistic Programming (NLP)**

This is the most advanced type of hypnosis and should only be performed by a well-trained hypnotherapist. I am saying this because later on, we will see how you can do self-hypnosis. NLP is a method of hypnosis that is used to treat severe addictions and other problems like phobias. It is the kind of hypnosis that reprograms your brain.

For instance, if you always smoke while having a morning cup of coffee, your mind pairs the two activities as activities that must be done simultaneously but with NLP, the brain dissociates the two activities and therefore you won't have the urge to smoke while having coffee.

Hypnosis Versus Meditation

There is a thin line between hypnosis and meditation. Most people assume that they are the same thing but that is not so. Therefore, it is important for you to know the difference so that you do your self-hypnosis the correct way.

Different purposes

Self-hypnosis is all about stimulating specific behavioral changes and its main mode is evoking positive thoughts and ideas into your subconscious. This is actually a unique way of getting your mind to relax. Meditation is meant to relax the mind completely. Meditation is training your mind to relax and involves freeing the mind from any thoughts. Hypnosis has specific objectives.

Action versus relaxation

Self-hypnosis helps you address particular issues and therefore you go beyond relaxing the mind as opposed to meditation. Hypnosis stimulates the relaxed subconscious to go after a perceived change while meditation is all about relishing the experience of a peaceful subconscious.

The main difference between the two practices lies in the objective and goal that you are pursuing.

Since both methods rely on relaxation, it can be easily concluded that meditation is the gateway to hypnosis.

Similarities between Meditation and Self Hypnosis

The two methods have several similarities. We already saw the first one and that is relaxation. There is also need for breathing and visualization in order to enter the hypnotic trance state. The two methods can be used to help in therapy or dealing with mental and physical health problems.

The only main difference that we can conclude about the two methods is that while self-hypnosis is set towards a change in your behavior, meditation is aimed at deep relaxation.

CHAPTER 2

HOW HYPNOSIS WORKS

Many theories try to explain the mechanics of hypnosis and try to make sense of the whole process but before looking on how it works, maybe the first question should be if hypnosis really works. Research going back to decades shows that hypnosis is greatly effective and can be used to treat a variety of conditions.

The June 2007 Journal of Pediatrics showed how the process helped reduce the duration and pain of headaches in children. There is also a study by Frank Schmidt showing how hypnosis is three times more effective when it comes to quitting the habit of smoking. This is better than nicotine replacement.

The theories that try to explain how the results are achieved state that hypnosis results in changes in how your brain works. The message is that hypnosis works by passing messages to your unconscious mind. The conscious mind is what you might refer to as the thinking you (as you read this sentence, you are doing so consciously). The unconscious mind on the other hand is in charge of all the autonomic processes that take place inside your body. These are the processes that you never have to think about before they happen for instance breathing, the beating of the heart, cell regeneration, or blood pressure. The subconscious is in charge of our emotions, habits and how we respond to our environment.

The conscious mind is more critical, analytical, and logical. It is the part of the mind that is constantly making value decisions. For instance, you may make a conscious decision that you will not be having a midnight snack but truth is that it is not that part of the brain responsible for that habit. The unconscious mind is more flexible and therefore more accepting. It is the part of your mind that normally takes things literally. As mentioned before, hypnosis works by leaving out the critical consciousness and communicating directly to the unconscious in a language that it understands. The language can be a metaphor, pattern, or association.

So, the unconscious part of your mind is what's in charge. The process of hypnosis works by updating your unconscious mind with new and more helpful information. Think of it as reprogramming a computer so that it can perform faster and much better.

Now that the unconscious mind is in charge of autonomic bodily functions then it should also be noted that hypnosis could bring about desired physical results. It is all about shaping perceptions by dealing directly with the seat of all that affects us that is the unconscious. The deep relaxation and focusing exercises that are involved in hypnosis help to calm and subdue your conscious mind to ensure that it takes a fairly less active role in your thinking. So in essence, you are still aware of what's happening when you are hypnotized but in this case, your conscious mind has taken a backseat to let your subconscious mind to take the reign. So hypnosis essentially enables you to allow the hypnotist to work directly with the subconscious such that they can make whichever suggestions they want. You can think of hypnosis as having the power to open a sort of control panel to your brain. So if your subconscious takes charge, you start feeling freer and are likely to be more creative especially given that the conscious mind is often the one that filters everything such that you 'know your limits'. Therefore, when you are hypnotized, your 'limit control' is sort of turned off. That's why you are bound to do some things that you would not ordinarily do because the conscious mind is ideally not filtering information that you are receiving from the subconscious. Since the hypnotists' suggestions go directly to the subconscious and are relayed without filtering, that's why you react sort of automatically to the suggestions and impulses as if you are just responding to your very own thoughts. Well, there are obviously things you won't do since the subconscious mind has some form of consciousness like the survival instinct and its own ideas so you won't just agree to everything including the dangerous ones. And since the subconscious mind usually regulates the different bodily sensations like sight, touch, taste and the different emotional feelings, when the 'command center' to your subconscious mind is under the control of the hypnotist, you can easily get trigger for these feelings so that you can experience things even when they don't exist in reality simply because the command is coming from the subconscious. For instance, you will feel your tongue fill the mouth etc. When this is coupled with the fact that the subconscious is also the storehouse of all the memories, this means that you or the hypnotist can access various past events that you probably had forgotten to help you to solve whatever problems you might have associated with what's in your memory especially because the hypnotist can suggest whatever changes they need to make to your subconscious to create what you would think of as 'false memories'.

Note: A hypnotist cannot just hypnotize you. You also have a role to play in the process:

✓ For starters, you need to have the desire to be hypnotized

✓ You should also believe that you can be hypnotized

✓ And must feel comfortable and relaxed

Before you are hypnotized, the hypnotist will probably test your willingness and capacity to be hypnotized. For instance, they might say something like 'relax your shoulders and arms completely' then move on to suggest something that would logically not be possible like 'picture yourself being weightless'. Depending on your personality and your mental state, a session can take anywhere between a few minutes to over 30minutes.

Depths of Hypnosis

There are different depths of hypnosis, which a person can enter. When you are in a state of hypnosis, the depths of hypnosis would fluctuate and as long as you don't go into the somnambulistic state, you would be fine but if you drift into the somnambulistic state, you would be too relaxed to react to commands given by the hypnotist and wouldn't be able to achieve much from the session.

There are four depths of hypnosis and they are:

1. **The Hypnoidal State (Waking State):** This is the first depth of hypnosis. It occurs immediately you start the session. It is much similar to that state that you get into prior to your sleep or just before you wake up.

2. **The Lethargic State (Light Trance State)**: This is the second depth of hypnosis and is also known as the light trance state. At this stage, you feel quite Lethargic and you may begin to experience something known as Rapid Eye Movement (R.E.M), where there is flickering of the eyelids and movement of the eyeballs. At this stage, you would be going into a deeper level of trance and would be more responsive to commands from the hypnotist than when you were in the waking state.

3. **The Cataleptic Trance State (The Medium State)**: At this stage, you would feel completely detached from the things happening in your surroundings. When you get out of the session, you may have a faint or no memory of things that happened in your surroundings from this point. You still respond to commands and are conscious but you would be deeply focused on the subject of the hypnosis and less focused on the happenings around you.

4. **The Somnambulistic State (Deep State):** This is a very deep state of hypnosis and is sometimes called the "Coma state'. Very few people can get into this state, which is characterized by feelings of total bliss and euphoria. In this state, you are completely unaware of your surroundings or events around. As such, there is likely to be a problem if such things pose a threat to your safety. At the somnambulistic state, you only experience things that you wish to experience.

Note: If you are skeptical about having someone hypnotize you, you can do it yourself. We will discuss how to do that later in the book.

When doing hypnosis on yourself, there are four steps that you must follow.

- The first step is motivation. Unless you have a good solid reason as to why you are engaging in hypnosis, you should not go ahead with the process because it will all be in vain.

- The next step is relaxation. Relax your mind so that you can easily switch it from the conscious to the sub conscious.

- The third step is concentration whereby you need to make your mind focus on a specific thing especially images so that you can create mental energy that is required for the hypnosis.

- The final step is directing. This step is very important if you have certain goals to achieve. In the state of your hypnosis, you will visualize these goals and see yourself achieving them.

For you to practice hypnosis, check out some of the following hypnosis techniques:

Eye fixation or fixed gaze induction

This is probably what you've seen in movies where hypnotists wave something like a pocket watch in front of a subject. The idea here is to get the subject to focus intently on the object in question to the extent that they tune out any other stimuli. And once the focus is achieved, it then becomes easy for the hypnotist to talk in a low tone to lull the subject into full relaxation. While this method was quite popular in the past, it is no longer very popular.

Progressive relaxation and imagery:

The technique is quite popular especially among psychiatrists. For this to be done, all the hypnotist needs to do is to speak to the subject in a slow and soothing voice to bring the subject to full relaxation and focus in order to ease the subject into a hypnotic trance. Self-hypnosis (to be discussed in a bit) uses this technique.

In this technique, the main idea is to overload the mind with firm (but sudden) commands. The logic is that commands that are more forceful are move 'hypnotizing' or convincing enough. In essence, they actually 'force' the subject to surrender all their consciousness over the situation at hand. It is very common among stage hypnotists especially because the fact that the subject is in front of an audience makes them want to obey (they are susceptible) any commands that the hypnotist issues.

The loss of balance technique

Always done by mothers when they want to lull babies to sleep, this strategy usually creates a sense of loss of equilibrium with the use of slow rhythmic rocking.

Well, all the explanations above seem all good. But how can they really help you in your day to day life? We will discuss all that in the next chapter.

CHAPTER 3

WHAT BENEFITS CAN YOU GET FROM HYPNOSIS?

Hypnosis holds many benefits for you especially in areas of mental, emotional and physical health. Hypnosis can even boost creativity and success as you would see below as we discuss some of the famous users of hypnosis.

Famous Users of Hypnosis

Hypnosis is not for the weak minded or unintelligent people as most people are wrongly led to believe. Many famous and successful people were known users of hypnosis. Some of them include:

Albert Einstein: Albert Einstein is one of the most popular and intelligent people to have walked the face of the earth. He was a known user of hypnosis. He regularly used hypnosis to relax and think deeply. One of his most famous theories "The theory of relativity" was even created in a state of hypnosis.

Sir Winston Churchill: Sir Winston Churchill was another famous user of hypnosis. He was known to use hypnosis to relieve the stress that came with his position as a prime minister and to stay awake during meetings during the Second World War.

Thomas Edison: Thomas Edison was the famous inventor of the light bulb. He was also a user of self-hypnosis.

Henry Ford: Henry Ford of the popular Ford Motors also used hypnosis on a regular basis.

Phil Jackson: Phil Jackson was coach of the L.A Lakers and the Chicago Bulls. He regularly used hypnosis with his teams, which included some of the most successful players today like Michael Jordan, Shaq O'Neal and Kobe Bryant.

Mozart: Mozart, the famous composer composed one of his most famous pieces "The Opera Cosi Fan Tutte" in a state of hypnosis.

The list of celebrities, who are regular users of hypnosis and have derived numerous benefits from the use of hypnosis, is endless. Some of them have used it to quit smoking, some have used it to boost productivity and some have used it to increase their levels of creativity. Let's learn more about the benefits of hypnosis in detail:

Benefits of Hypnosis

1. Hypnosis is beneficial in the treatment of addictions. Whether it is drug or food addiction, hypnosis can be used to kick out negative habits. This involves the use of the three different types of hypnosis. The role of hypnosis in fighting addictions is to help you regain control of your thoughts and actions and enable you to make smart choices. Hypnosis does not only help stop addictions permanently but it also helps alleviate the physical symptoms of addiction.

2. Hypnosis helps in losing weight and keeping it off. Studies have shown that hypnotherapy is 30% more effective than just relying on dieting alone.

3. Hypnosis helps in managing chronic pain. People suffering from conditions such as migraines or arthritis usually undergo tremendous pain. Hypnosis comes in when drugs and diet have not helped in managing the condition. It is not healthy to be popping pills every now and then because that can also lead to an addiction whereby you cannot live without painkillers.

4. Hypnosis helps in reducing stress. Stress is an underlying factor for many health conditions like high blood pressure, heart disease, diabetes, sleep disorders, and obesity. You need to relax and this can be made possible through hypnosis and other techniques like meditation and yoga.

5. Hypnosis helps us to deal with our past. This is especially true when it comes to dealing with childhood issues like abuse, low self-esteem, PTSD and others. This process allows you to look into those issues and replace the negative messages with positive ones.

6. Hypnosis helps cure sleep disorders. Sleep disorders bring about many health complications including addiction, obesity and ultimately stress and depression. Most of these sleep disorders are due to psychological matters. Hypnosis helps to treat the psychological root of the sleep problem.

7. Hypnosis promotes deep relaxation. When you relax, you become a much more productive person.

8. Hypnosis helps in behavior change. There are people who have anger issues and others who are too emotional.

Hypnosis can help change negative behavior patterns into positive ones. With hypnosis, it is easy to identify the underlying issues and deal with them so that they no longer have a hold on you.

9. Hypnosis helps you remember. All memories are buried somewhere in the subconscious mind. So if there is something you want to remember, then hypnosis will pop it out for you.

10. Hypnosis is effective in the treatment of anxiety and depression. If you are tired of using antidepressants, hypnosis can help. Hypnosis helps to eliminate what triggers such negative feelings.

11. Self-hypnosis changes your mindset for a successful and happier you: Stress, anxiety, and depression are all related mental problems. You will therefore have to get rid of them before they can destroy you. Self-hypnosis helps you achieve this. Let me explain this: When you go through life carrying all its burdens, then negative thoughts will overshadow you. You will never think that anything good could ever happen to you and therefore end up being a pessimist. Negative thoughts do not just affect your mind but they also affect your body. Some studies have shown that water molecules changed their form, become unbalanced and take on an unpleasant shape when in an environment of unpleasant thoughts and the exact opposite happens in an environment filled with positive thoughts.

Now that you know the truth, let us see how you can set your mind ready so that you only incorporate positive thoughts into your life.

Your subconscious has no fixed morality and it varies from person to person depending on your conditioning and memory. If something bad happens to you as a result of an action you did, then your mind will isolate that action as being negative. However, it is important to know that one rejection does not mean that the same action will yield the same result.

While you can easily say that you will use positive affirmations to nurture happiness by seeing the glass as half full as opposed to half empty, the truth is that this might not always be certain that you will change your mind set. The truth is you must get your subconscious mind involved in making the necessary changes in your life if you truly want to see sustainable change. You can think of negativity as a dark night whereby your vision is obscured. Self-hypnosis is the only tool that can bring back the light of positivity and eliminate the negativity in your life.

We mentioned somewhere that hypnosis helps fight anxiety, stress, and depression. So how does it do that? We will cover that in the next chapter.

CHAPTER 4

HOW HYPNOSIS HELPS CURE DE-PRESSION, ANXIETY AND STRESS AND BRING HAPPINESS

As stated before, most people usually go for an over the counter prescription when it comes to dealing with stress, depression and anxiety but actually, this is not dealing with the root problem. When we take pills, we are simply dealing with the symptoms and looking for a shortcut, which might end up leaving us worse than we were. Actually, drugs simply suppress the symptoms but they don't really solve the underlying problem.

Self-hypnosis is one of the effective and simple ways to deal with the above health problems, since it enables you to change the way you feel and think.

Our minds are like gardens and the thoughts we have are the seeds. Good thoughts are like good crops while bad ones are like weeds thus yielding tension and stress. Stress alters our body and mind.

Almost everyone has been stressed but the issue is not the situation but how we react to the situation itself. Your mind commands the thoughts that you have. Constructive thoughts give us confidence that helps us attain our goals while destructive thoughts achieve the opposite. When stress is not managed, it compresses like gas waiting to explode.

There is good stress and bad stress. Good stress gives you the adrenalin rush to act towards your goals but unmanaged stress has the ability to lead to depression and other health complications like ulcers, asthma, and stroke.

Hypnosis is one of the lesser known, less practiced effective methods of managing stress, and yet it is one of the oldest and best techniques known to man when it comes to dealing with stress. It is not magical or mystic; instead, it is all about letting out our emotions and feelings that are troubling us. Yes, you will be in a trance state but you will still be focused. While in this state, you will bring the desired goals into memory and then keep on repeating these ideas so that when you are stressed again, you will not be overwhelmed.

Hypnosis is much faster and effective in dealing with stress compared to meditation and yoga. Additionally, self-hypnosis is easier than yoga or any other exercise. This means it can work even for those who are limited physically. Another thing is that it has no side effects as compared to some medical and herbal therapies. The Ericksonian is quite good since it allows the use of metaphors, which enhance the state of hypnosis. The NLP method is more powerful whereby the stress causing factors are triggered to make you relax instead of being tense.

The Role Of Imagery

Imagery plays a greater role in self-hypnosis. You need to visualize yourself in a better place and believe it. The health benefits of imagery are great and that is why they are used in fighting stress, depression, and anxiety. Those who make use of imagery usually experience a greater state of relaxation and envisioning and they do so with a deep detail that associates with all their senses.

The pros

Imagery gives relaxation, wisdom, and insight. It is a stress relieving method of therapy that can be done almost anywhere.

✓ Tip: Guided imagery is essential in ensuring that you are totally relaxed during hypnosis.

The cons

It takes some time to master how to automatically have guided imagery.

Guided Imagery Hypnosis

Time Required: 10-15 Minutes

Get into a comfortable position, like one you would use for meditation or self-hypnosis. If a lying-down position would likely put you to sleep, opt for a cross-legged position (lotus position-shown below), or recline in a comfortable chair.

Get comfortable and breathe deeply with your eyes closed. Once you are relaxed, begin to see yourself in the most relaxed environment you could ever be in for instance the ocean or up in the sky. As you are imagining, try to incorporate all your senses; how does the place look, what is the aura, how does it feel, do you hear anything?

Stay in that place for as long as you need to and enjoy yourself. Let nothing stress you.

When you have had enough, you can come back to reality by counting back from twenty or ten. You will have taken a mini vacation without having to leave the room.

Tips of getting imagery during self-hypnosis

Make use of soft ambient sounds that will help enhance your imagery. Some nice accapella music should do the trick or maybe classical music.

Do set an alarm just in case you lose track of time or fall asleep.

What You Need

- ✓ Some quiet time
- ✓ Privacy
- ✓ An alarm clock

CHAPTER 5

HOW TO PREPARE YOURSELF FOR A HYPNOSIS SESSION TO GUARANTEE GREATER EFFECTIVENESS

Failing to prepare is preparing to fail. Therefore, if you want your self-hypnosis session to be successful, you will need to do certain things to ensure that the whole process is effective.

Wear Comfortable Clothing

As much as this is obvious, we still had to mention to emphasize how important it is for you to be completely comfortable and relaxed during the whole experience. Ensure that there is nothing poking you or there is nothing too tight or makes you lose focus.

Eat something an hour before the process

This is important because when blood sugar levels go down, you cannot get much done. For you to achieve a deeper state during hypnosis, your blood sugar level should be stable.

Note: Kindly stay away from stimulants for about two hours before your hypnosis session.

Write down dreams in a dream journal

This is because dreams help you with your imagery and imagery is the main tool during hypnosis.

Write out the reasons why you need hypnosis

Get a piece of paper or notebook and write down all the valid reasons why you should do hypnosis. This is because you need to be willing to go through it for hypnosis to work.

Write down your goals

This can be the same as the list above but it is always good to have a separate list as to what you desire to achieve. This enables you to easily pick the most urgent goal to work on.

Tell a trusted friend what you are up to

Let them know what your goal is because it is good to have someone who will keep pushing you to achieve it and you will be accountable to them.

Keep a journal in order to keep track of your sessions

Not all the sessions will be similar. Some might even fade away faster than others so write down some notes and see what kind of progress you are making.

Sometimes the things you experience in hypnosis fade away quickly; thus, it is advisable to write down notes and keep track of your progress.

Have an open mind

Be open to new experiences. With hypnosis, you never know what will happen next unless you experience it.

Always hope for the best outcome

Know that your mind is very powerful. It directs the actions you take so that you can actualize your goals.

How To Enhance The Entire Experience

So how can you ensure that you have a good hypnosis session to overcome stress, anxiety and feel happy? Here are some ideas on how to make this possible:

- Don't just chant; mean what you say. Believe in yourself and the actions that you do because this is the only way to derive the full benefits.

- Physical enhancement; You can achieve this by engaging in certain exercises during hypnosis like wiggling your toes or even visualizing your arms getting heavier.

- Make use of your environment; Play some music or have a timer. The sound of rain or water can also help put you at ease.

- Be positive. Hypnosis helps you to become the person whom you want to become. Visualize yourself being the best version of yourself. Remember that you can suggest anything and your mind will believe it so whatever version of yourself you want your mind to believe, feel free to suggest it without fear or doubt.

CHAPTER 6

HOW TO HYPNOTIZE YOURSELF TO FIGHT DEPRESSION

Self-hypnosis is an act of hypnotizing oneself using your own voice or thoughts. The affirmations or positive thoughts are founded on your rational thinking so as to overcome anxiety and stress. You will repeat these affirmations over and over again into your subconscious so that you are motivated to achieve your goals and desires. The process can also be done without affirmations depending on your needs.

Self-hypnosis will help your body relax so as to relieve anxiety and subside cortisol the stress hormone. You will free your mind from unpleasant thoughts thus changing your outlook on life and becoming more focused.

Obviously, this method is cheaper since you will not need to consult a hypnotherapist.

The Steps

1. Close your eyes and rid your mind of any negative feelings like fear, anxiety, or stress. At the beginning, it is hard to stop yourself from thinking and thoughts might keep on intruding. If this is your case, then do not force the thoughts out of your mind. Rather, just observe impartially and they will slip away. The other alternative

is to pick something (e.g. the wall) and focus on it. Focus on one point and let your eyelids feel heavier and heavier. Let them close without opening.

2. Recognize the tension that is in your body. You will start with your toes and imagine the tension flowing down and leaving your body. Imagine the same process for each part of your body and visualize your body beginning to become lighter and lighter. The whole process starts by you relaxing your toes then the feet going up until you get to the head. Make use of imagery techniques (you can visualize/imagine the relaxing or soothing feel of water, or the blue sky) that makes you feel soothed and comfortable.

3. Slow deep breaths. When you are exhaling, see tension and negativity leaving your body as a dark cloud then when you inhale, see the same cloud coming back bright and fully filled with energy and life. Always concentrate on your five senses.

4. Appreciate that you are now truly relaxed. Simply imagine that you are at the top of a flight of ten stairs and that each step you take leads you to water. As you take every step, let your feet feel the sensation and once you step into the water, imagine how cool and refreshing it feels. Imagine the water to be an oasis of purity and cleanliness. Simply get into the water and drift in forgetting all your worries and troubles.

5. Start feeling a floating sensation. This is the point where you are not feeling anything and all that you are experiencing is the sensation of floating. At times, you may feel like you are spinning. If this is not the case, then try again but much slower. It is after this state when you can now move on to address your issues. You will start by speaking to yourself in both the present and future tense. Picture three boxes that are under the water and that you have to swim and get them. Once you get to there, open them one by one, and narrate to yourself what happens. Say words like "As I open the box, I feel a bright light covering me." Avoid negative statements. Say words such as, "My pain is drifting away or I am calm and peaceful."

6. Repeat the above positive statements as many times as possible. Free yourself in the water. Open the boxes and find treasure. This is in the form of new confidence or strength. Also, do let all the tension drift away. Set your imagination free.

7. Prepare to exit the hypnotic state. Imagine the water levels becoming lower as you begin to rise up the stairs. You may feel heavier when on the sixth step but when this happens, keep telling yourself the positive statements and soon, you will be lighter.

8. Once you are up the stairs, wait a few minutes before you open your eyes. You may visualize yourself opening a door to a new world. Do this slowly so that your eyes open naturally or you can simply count from ten and then open your eyes.

CHAPTER 7

HOW TO HYPNOTIZE YOURSELF TO STOP ANXIETY

We all suffer from anxiety from time to time so it's safe to say that anxiety is a normal occurrence. However, anxiety attacks are not normal. People who suffer from anxiety attacks are unable to think rationally because their rational minds are under siege.

Hypnosis can help you work on your subconscious mind so that you are able to calm down and rationalize rather than remaining in a state of anxiety or panic. So how do you hypnotize yourself to overcome anxiety? Let's learn how to do that:

The Steps

Create Self-Affirmation Statements: Hypnosis is much more effective when you work with self-affirmation statements. They should be kept simple but they must also be genuine and honest. For instance, you could use statements like: "I am in control", "I can handle this" ,"I am brave", "I am confident".

Ensure that you use present tenses when creating your self-affirmation statements.

Get into a Comfortable Position: Self-hypnosis for anxiety works with progressive relaxation techniques. First, you get into a comfortable position and start relaxing all your muscles from the toes to your feet then your ankles, calves, thighs, buttocks, abdomen, fingers, hands, wrists, elbows, shoulders, neck, face and lastly, your held. Hold each muscle tight for a few seconds and then release before going on to another muscle. As you work on the muscles, eliminate all other thoughts from your mind and focus solely on the muscles you are working on.

Find an Object of Focus: Choose an object that you can focus on. This could be anything but it must be in a comfortable position such that you are able to look upwards slightly. Also, you shouldn't force your focus; if you become distracted with random thoughts, just allow them pass and then slowly redirect your focus on the object.

Breathe deeply and slowly: Start by consciously slowing down your breath. Start taking deep and slow breaths then count your breaths as you breath. Make sure your focus is still on the object.

Repeat Your Positive Statements: Start counting backwards from 10. Tell yourself that you would have reached your subconscious state and be hypnotized by the time you count to 1. Then start repeating your positive statements. As you say them, picture yourself saying them. For instance, you can picture yourself saying them to something or someone who frightens you.

Pinch your Hands: As you make your positive statements, pinch yourself at the back of your hands. This pinch helps you remember to say your affirmative statements even when you enter into your subconscious state.

Come out of the Process: Start coming out of the hypnosis state by reversing the process. Count from 1 to 10 and keep repeating your positive statements as you count. Then open your eyes when you get to 10 and start taking deep breaths. Do this for a few minutes before getting up.

For you to properly master and enjoy the art of hypnosis, for anxiety relief, you have to practice as often as you can. You can start with the help of a professional who would guide you through the process and show you how it is done then when you have fully mastered the art, you can begin to do it yourself at home.

CHAPTER 8

HOW TO HYPNOTIZE YOURSELF TO REDUCE STRESS

Hypnosis is one of the most powerful tools that are being used to fight stress today. Stress can cause severe health problems for you because stress unnecessarily saps the body of its energy in readiness to defend itself from situations and circumstances that are sometimes imaginary. Overload of stress can also spiral into other health problems such as insomnia, high blood pressure, headaches and other health problems.

You can combine self-hypnosis with a number of other stress-relieving techniques in order to achieve the maximum results.

Hypnosis helps you get into a deeply relaxed state, helps you relieve tension and triggers the relaxation response in you, which are all necessary for stress relief.

To do self-hypnosis for stress-relief, you should follow the steps that have been outlined below:

Steps

Allocate between five to thirty free minutes for the session.

Search for a calm and quiet place where you would be free from distractions.

Settle into a comfortable position. You could choose to sit with your legs crossed as recline. Do whatever is comfortable for you but ensure that you do not fall asleep in the process.

Decide on what you want to achieve with the session and create positive statements out of it.

Start taking deep breaths. Don't raise your shoulders as you inhale. Instead, expand your abdomen and feel the oxygen spreading from your chest to your arms, your fingers down to your legs and toes then exhale. Imagine yourself exhaling all the stress and anxiety that you feel as you exhale. Continue to take these deep breaths.

Within your mind, search for an environment that relaxes you. Imagine yourself going into that environment and further and further into it. For instance, you could think of yourself walking down a very long corridor or walking deep into the woods. Continue to focus on this visualization and slowly, you would get into an altered/hypnotized state. An altered state feels like daydreaming or deep concentration.

Remain in this state until you feel completely relaxed and far from your regular life. At this state, you can now start repeating your positive affirmations.

Do this for a few minutes and then make the intention to get out of your hypnotic state and end the session.

Start coming out of the process by counting from one to ten, then slowly open your eyes.

Relax for a few minutes then get up.

Tip: You can play some soft music or use some scented candles to introduce some aromatherapy. Aromatherapy, self-hypnosis and music are a perfect combination for stress relief.

CHAPTER 9

AM I HYPNOTIZED YET? HOW TO KNOW IF YOU ARE IN A TRANCE AND HOW TO GET OUT

The word trance means a state where a person is not fully conscious and most of the times, they are unable to respond to what is going on around them. Being in a hypnotic trance is actually forgetting everything else and super-focusing on the subconscious and responding to only what is coming from the subconscious as opposed to the conscious mind. Everything else is tuned off. The result is intense relaxation and willingness to accept whatever information you get during this state. But you must note that you are still in control of all yourself thus your brain can reject what does not please it. In this state, the following will happen:

1. You are able to do physical actions, which you have no control of.

2. You are able to alter stubborn ideas or beliefs that you may have.

3. You will experience physical and mental healing e.g. stopping smoking or overcoming stress.

So the big question here is; how do you know that you are in a trance or you were in a trance? There are several indicators but you will have to have sharp senses so as to understand the changes that are taking place in your system. Some signs will easily manifest themselves while some won't.

Some noticeable signs that you are or were in a trance include:

Physiological Changes

- Your head drops as if you are falling asleep

- Breathing changes

- Changes on the skin; Change in complexion and you may feel warmer or colder than usual.

- Shoulders are slumped

- Change in muscle tone

Eye

- Less blinking

- Tears may flow

- Fixed on a single gaze

- Twitching of the eyelids/ rapid eye movement

- Softened face

- Facial muscle change

Other signs

- Pulse and heart rate slows down

- Twitching of your body and lips

- Licking your lips

- Swallowing

Apart from these signs, there are also other signs that may occur as we go on with our daily routine. For instance, you may reminisce memories from the past or as you cook, you remember a certain flavor.

How to Get Out Of Trance without Watering Down The Benefits

So how do you get out now that you know how to get into a trance? You need a method that will not interfere with the incredible positive effects of the hypnosis.

Simply tell yourself that when you reach one, you will open your eyes and be totally awake and feel refreshed. After saying this to yourself, start counting slowing from five to one.

Hypnotic trance is a very powerful tool in overcoming problems in life or overcoming our fears and helping us deal with various situations around us. For it to be more effective, do it often because practice makes perfect.

CHAPTER 10

FAQ ABOUT HYPNOSIS

In this chapter, we are going to reveal all the answers we can get to the questions that you might have about hypnosis.

Can anyone be hypnotized?

The answer to this is yes; everyone can be hypnotized to a certain extent. This is because there are those of us who are more susceptible than others are. There are three categories of measuring how susceptible you are to hypnosis namely: highs, mediums and lows. Eighty percent of people are in the mediums category while ten percent are classified as lows. The rest are highs.

Is hypnosis dangerous?

Hypnosis is like an induced trance like state but the intention is to give the individual intense awareness of the present moment. Most of the times, TV portrays hypnosis in the negative where the individual loses control over their behavior when hypnotized but actually, that is not true.

Experts at Mayo Clinic have stated that even when you are in a trance, you will always be aware of what is happening and even remember it afterwards.

According to Dr. Andrew Weil, a physician and leading expert in integrative medicine, hypnosis is a safe and effective procedure and that practicing it is beneficial. He believes that the field has not been researched well since the research community hasn't taken hypnosis seriously.

The National Center for Complementary and Integrative Health indicates that hypnotherapy has been studied for various conditions such as headaches, anxiety, pain control, quitting smoking and irritable bowel syndrome. They have cited research that suggests clinical hypnosis can help some women with hot flashes. There is also evidence suggesting that hypnosis relaxation therapy could help with pain management.

Most people think that hypnosis takes away control but actually, what it does is to enhance it. The therapist simply guides you into a hypnotic trance mostly after discussing about your thoughts, goals, and expectations.

Can hypnosis make me do things I don't want to do?

The answer here is no. Even during hypnosis, you still have the power to say no or yes to suggestions. The issue is that when you say yes to some suggestions, then even if they occur, you might feel as if they take place without your control.

Is hypnosis like sleep?

No. hypnosis is not like sleep. When observing a person under hypnosis, it may look like they are sleeping but actually, they are awake and there is quite some brain activity happening.

How does being in a hypnotic trance feel like?

The answer here is that the whole experience is entirely different for everyone. No one experiences the same thing as another person. It is all different. There are those who feel light while others feel heavy. Additionally, what works for you might not work for another person.

Can a person get stuck in hypnosis?

There is no evidence to show that people can get stuck in hypnosis. The worst that can happen is you falling asleep and waking up without being hypnotized.

What conditions can hypnosis treat?

Most researchers don't think of hypnosis as a treatment but actually, it does help treat several health problems like depression, pain, addictions and anxiety conditions.

Are some words more suggestive than others are?

It is encouraged that we be careful with the words we use during hypnosis but there is no telling which word is more suggestive than the other is. All that is accepted currently is that how well you respond to hypnosis all depends on your individual characteristics like willingness, absorption, or susceptibility.

Is hypnosis ever a one-session "quick fix" for a problem?

It all depends on what the problem is. The more serious the problem is, the more the number of sessions that might be required.

Will my secrets be revealed?

Hypnosis is not a lie detecting machine/session. During the session, you are still in control and therefore are able to decide what to say and what not to say.

CHAPTER 11

DO THIS FOR ONE MINUTE

We have seen how you can go about self-hypnosis but maybe you need more sessions and you have very little time to spare. Well, there is a way you can be doing self-hypnosis within a minute and get great results. According to Sharon Basaraba, a Healthy Aging Expert, the following steps can help you out.

Self-Hypnosis: A One-Minute Method

- Sit or lie comfortably

- Close your eyes

- Imagine holding an energy ball.

- See yourself squeezing the ball.

- Visualize that the harder you squeeze the ball the more it resists the squeeze

- Assure yourself that the harder you squeeze the deeper you go.

- Feel that you are going deep inside.

- Give a suggestion to yourself. Say that you feel energizing or loving.

- See the outcome you desire being actualized.

- Feel the positive feelings associated with the positive outcome.

After a while, tell yourself you are coming back better and refreshed then slowly open your eyes. Do not be discouraged because you did not see something miraculous happen the first time you do self-hypnosis.

Then slowly open your eyes.

CONCLUSION

Everyone wants to be happy but at times there is something that hinders us from enjoying the sunshine like everyone else. Self-hypnosis is a self-help method that helps you to regain back control over your life and the results that you want to see. It is not hard at all; simply be motivated and you will be on the right path to being happy again with nothing holding you down since now you have the key.

MY FREE GIFT TO YOU!

As a way of saying thank you for purchasing my book, I'd like to send you an exclusive gift that will help with using Hypnosis for your health.

Hypnotherapy Health is a quick and exclusive guide on how to use audio hypnotherapy to improve your life and make money. Check it out and bring the best version of yourself out NOW!

I am giving you this FREE BONUS to thank you for being such an awesome reader and to make sure I give you all the value that I can in your mission of improving your life with hypnosis!

To get your FREE gift, type in the link below and follow the steps & I'll send it to your e-mail address right away.

www.hypnosiskindlebook.com

Thank you again for purchasing this book!

I hope this book was able to help you to understand how to hypnotize yourself to overcome stress, depression, anxiety and be happy.

The next step is to implement what you have learnt

Finally, if you enjoyed this book, would you be kind enough to leave a review for this book on Amazon?

Thank you and good luck!